# The Christmas Angels

The story of angels at Christmas

Matthew 1–2 and Luke 1–2 for children

Written by Sara Hartman

Illustrated by Linda Graves

CONCORDIA PUBLISHING HOUSE • SAINT LOUIS

God's holy army of angels
Sang with joy as creation began,
As God created the heavens and earth
And, in His own image, man.

An angel blocked the entrance to Eden
When Adam and Eve fell from grace.
But God promised to send a Savior
To redeem the whole human race.

Angels served and protected God's people
Throughout the Old Testament years.
God had exciting new tasks for the angels
As the time for the Savior grew near.

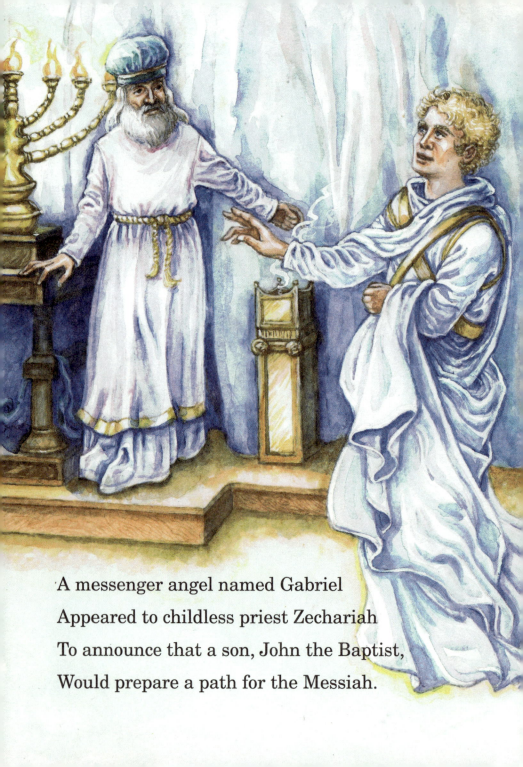

A messenger angel named Gabriel
Appeared to childless priest Zechariah
To announce that a son, John the Baptist,
Would prepare a path for the Messiah.

Gabriel appeared again in Nazareth,
To a young virgin girl named Mary.
He told her she had found favor with God
And of the miracle child she would carry.

Joseph, a hardworking carpenter,
Had planned to make Mary his wife.
But when he heard the news of the baby,
It upset his plans for their life.

As Joseph slept that night, God's angel
Then told him, "Do not be afraid;
Mary's child is of God. Name Him Jesus.
He is God's promise, so long ago made."

Joseph believed and took Mary as his wife.

Soon they traveled to Bethlehem

When Caesar ordered a Roman census,

But the inn there had no room to give them.

So baby Jesus was born in a stable.
As shepherds watched flocks nearby,
A heavenly host of angels appeared.
Their glory lit up the night sky.

"Do not be afraid; we have good news,"
An angel told the terrified men.
"The Savior is born in Bethlehem!"
Then they all sang a glorious hymn.

The angels left when their song was done,

And the shepherds rushed to see

That everything was as the angel had said.

And they worshiped on bended knee.

A bright star led Wise Men from the East
On a search for the King of the Jews.
They met wicked King Herod on the way,
Who felt threatened by their strange news.

The Wise Men found Jesus in Bethlehem,
Bowed down, and gave gifts from their packs.
Though they had pledged to report to Herod,
They followed a different route back.

Herod vowed to destroy the new King.

But an angel again saved the day

By telling Joseph in another dream

To take Mary and Jesus away.

They traveled to Egypt and lived there
Until Herod died; then a third angel dream
Led them home to fulfill the prophecy
That God's Son would be Nazarene.

Like the angels, we, too, can keep busy
Telling those we meet about Jesus' birth,
How He lived and died and rose again
For the sins of all people on earth.

Dear Parents,

Angels are an enduring symbol of Christmas and of God's p
vision for us, but popular culture usually misrepresents them.
love Clarence in the popular Christmas movie *It's a Wonderful L*
but Scripture does not tell us that people become angels when tl
die. We picture angels as delicate feminine creatures atop Christn
trees, but the Bible tells us that angels are powerful, even frig
ening. God tells us that angels are His created beings ("It was
hands that stretched out the heavens, and I commanded all th
host," Isaiah 45:12; "For by Him all things were created, in heav
and on earth, visible and invisible, whether thrones or dominions
rulers or authorities—all things were created through Him and
Him," Colossians 1:16), just as people are His created beings.

As this Arch Book emphasizes, the Bible tells us that angels ha
various roles, including giving praise to God and serving as His m
sengers. On your own or with your child, conduct a quick Inter
search of Bible passages that refer specifically to angels in th
roles, or look up these passages that describe angels giving glory
God: Psalm 148:2; Luke 2:13–14; Luke 15:10; Hebrews 1:6; Reve
tion 5:9–13. These passages identify angels as messengers: Dar
9:20–23; Daniel 10:5–21; Matthew 28:1–7; Luke 1:11–20; Acts 10:1

God's Word also tells us that angels are protectors, or guardia
Genesis 19:15–17; Psalm 91:11–12; Daniel 6:22; Matthew 26:53; A
5:18–19.

As you read this book, help your child learn to differentiate
tween what popular culture says about angels and what God t
us about them. Above all, help your child understand that just I
angels, our highest purpose is to give glory to God for His gift
Savior.

The Editor